The Alexia Foundation aspires

to give voice to social injustice,

to give voice to history,

and to give voice to cultural differences

so as to promote global understanding

through photojournalism.

Rebels in northern Uganda have kidnapped, most often at night, 12,000 children for use as soldiers, sex slaves and porters since June, 2002. "Night commuters," with sleeping mats on their heads, walk as many as three miles to their homes after spending the night in the safety of Kitgum city center. Photograph by Roger Lemoyne.

EYES ON THE WORLD

The Alexia Foundation for World Peace and Cultural Understanding

This book is dedicated to Alexia Tsairis (1968–1988),
taken from us by a terrorist's bomb aboard Pan Am Flight 103
over Lockerbie, Scotland.

ISBN: 0-9778816-0-1

contents

What a thrill it must be for winners of an Alexia scholarship or grant! Applicants for either must possess two key qualifications — top-notch photographic skills and a solid, well-researched proposal on an important topic.

The Alexia awards have proven to be one of today's most valuable photojournalism grants worldwide. Outlets for good photojournalism are diminishing in the marketplace, in part, perhaps, because readers may shy away from stories showing harsh reality. In addition, many photographers do not have the means to pursue their ideas.

The Alexia Foundation's mission is to provide those means.

High praise is due Aphrodite and Peter Tsairis, who started the program 16 years ago, and to Associate Professor at Syracuse University, David Sutherland, project coordinator.

Good photographers require extraordinary creativity in order to make exciting images. Each turn of the page of this book provides visual excitement. The hallmark of a fine photograph is its memorability. Memorable images appear on virtually every page. Most importantly, photographers must have something to say and they must know how to say it.

Matt Black, an early winner, recorded the nearly forgotten life of modern-day black sharecroppers in California. His photograph of one of the subjects standing in the doorway of the shack he called home is sure to grab and hold one's attention.

Peggy Peattie, another early winner, found her subject in South Carolina, at the time the only state to fly the Confederate flag. Her photographs tell the story of South Carolinians on both sides of the flag debate. Each image stays with you long after you turn the page.

In the essay by Marcus Bleasdale on the Chad-Cameroon pipeline project, we see a native woman sitting on a stool in her primitive home. On the floor is a shiny metal cooking pot, her compensation for giving the pipeline owners the right to build on her property. The value of the picture content speaks volumes.

The photographs in this book offer a powerful and emotional learning experience. The picture makers have something to say.

— Robert Gilka, former director of photography, National Geographic Magazine

When we established the student competition of the Alexia Foundation for World Peace and Cultural Understanding after our daughter Alexia was tragically caught in the web of international terrorism, we were determined to make sure it helped developing photojournalists do important work. We did not anticipate how enriching and healing it would be for us personally. To paraphrase a wonderful thought read somewhere long ago — the interconnectedness between people doing meaningful work halves sorrow and doubles joy. We are living testament that this is true.

On a cold, blustery Syracuse day in 1989, we sat in the student chairs of an empty classroom at the S.I. Newhouse School of Public Communications at Syracuse University with David Sutherland, her photography professor and mentor. In a few hours in that room, three people gave life to a lost photographer's legacy. "The Alexia," as the competition has come to be known, gives voice to the quest for important social documentary photojournalism. That was our mission.

Almost every picture story that crosses the sights of the Alexia competition judges has a component of hope. Hope is a lifeline. We get interested, excited, fascinated, reinvigorated. For hope is the road to survival.

Afterall, it was hope for the future that helped us survive the despair of our loss. At the annual judging of the Alexia Competitions at Syracuse University, that spirit of hopefulness is renewed by the quality of the images that are submitted and by the commitment and determination of the photographers. In its 16-year history, The Alexia Foundation for World Peace and Cultural Understanding has amassed a body of work with subjects from around the globe. To date, we have awarded over $500,000 in grants to 80 undergraduate photographers and 11 professionals.

This retrospective book, "Eyes on the World," represents a selection of photographic essays and images that identify and explain cultural differences and their political effects on our world community. Who can turn away from this book's cover image of the soulful gaze of Ami Vitale's photo of the 5-year-old girl crying after being ritually circumcised? You want to learn more.

We, at the Alexia Foundation, strive to find the images that will have a profound, socially significant impact — ones that will reinforce the power of photography to bring about change. The inscription on a plaque presented to us by the National Press Photographers Association reads, "In recognition of their promoting the dream of their daughter, Alexia: to bring the world closer together through documentary photography."

Our mission is to continue to develop affirmative photographers who are seeking to bridge the gaps that separate people. It is our charge to them. It is their mission to accomplish it.

— Peter Tsairis, MD and Aphrodite Thevos Tsairis

"It is important to photograph their

experiences now because theirs is a

universal story to so many zones of

conflict around the world,

stuggling for survival

in an increasingly shrinking world."

HEIDI BRADNER | pg 26

STRIFE | Consequence | Insight

to give voice to social injustice

Attempting to heal a terrorized nation

On May 25, 1997, the democratically-elected West African government in Sierra Leone was overthrown by a coalition of rebels. President Tejan Kabbah fled to exile in Guinea. The civil war raged on. Most of the civilians of Sierra Leone found themselves held hostage in this struggle between the different factions seeking power and control of Sierra Leone's natural resources, most notably, its diamonds. Fode Dabor, Sierra Leone's UN representative, believes the rebels finance their operations and buy arms by selling the diamonds they recover from mines in eastern Sierra Leone.

Cruelty and violence towards civilians is the rebels' calling card. They have mutilated hundreds of men, women and children by hacking off limbs. Some of the victims have been given letters warning President Kabbah, who was returned to office by African peacekeeping troops in March, 1998, that armed resistance will continue and no one is safe.

Barbara Crossette, of Refugees International, a Washington advocacy group, filed a chilling account of one multilated man's experience with his rebel captors. The rebels told the man, "You don't want a military government? You say you want a civilian government? Then we will have to cut off your hands. Then go to Tejan Kabbah and he will have to give you new hands."

Dabor calls the rebel tactics "atrocious." He said, "I've never seen this before. This is one of the most vicious rebel organizations in the world."

Internal Displaced People flee the rebels who systematically burn down villages. They usually head for Freetown. The refugees on this truck had nothing but the clothes they were wearing.

The rebels were known to chop off hands, and sometimes legs, with machetes. Mariatu Kamara, 14, from Port Loko, in the center of this photograph, hid in the bush with her two sisters and brother, at right, but all were caught and their hands were amputated.

The Westside Boys formed another faction in the war. They were often high on drugs and alcohol, what they called "morale boosters." They knew no loyalty and easily switched sides, one day fighting alongside the government soldiers and the next, taking hostages.

Young men and boys work for meager wages at a diamond mine under rebel control. If diamonds are found, the "owners" of the mine claim them. Women are forbidden to enter the mines.

Rebels line up to surrender their weapons and ammunition. The city of Khailahuna, a rebel
stronghold, was the last to disarm. Disarmament was conducted in collaboration with the U.N.

Once a peace accord was reached, the Sierra Leonean government enrolled all the different factions in military training at camps such as this one in Bemguema. The goal is to create a single, unified army and prevent street gangs, like the Westside boys, from emerging.

Amputees and their relatives live in huts made from sticks covered with plastic. In the rainy season, water splashes through the seams of the plastic sheets and everything gets soaked.

NEX T PAGE
Gibrilla Kam
to vote for F
her with a n

A woman c
Sierra Leor
became dis

A baby, suffering from malnutrition and infections, is one of many Internal Displaced People at a camp in Freetown, Sierra Leone. IDPs are completely dependent on aid from organizations such as the UN's world food program, Médecins Sans Frontiéres and the Red Cross.

Weary r[...]
Leone. [...]
in Freet[...]

A mother, homeless for the second time after an outbreak of hostilities between Abkhazia and Georgia, holds a candle near the portrait of her son, killed in the same conflict five years earlier.

A cradle of conflict and coexistence

The rugged Caucasus mountains form a magnificent treasure box of different faiths, languages and cultures but it is also a tinderbox which exploded into war seven times in seven years following the fall of the Soviet Union.

A succession of blazing conflicts has spread the width and length of the Caucasuses, starting in Georgia and culminating in the tragic and brutal war in Chechnya. What began as a blitzkrieg launched by a cavalier Kremlin, ended in a David versus Goliath defeat for the Russian giant, shocking the world and traumatizing both nations. The war in this tiny Caucasian republic reached scales of destruction the world had not seen since World War II.

The Caucasus mountains are home to hundreds of clans and ethnic minorities. To subdue its peoples took 300 years and all the might of the Russian czars. Mother Russia claimed her bloodstained "Prize of the Caucasuses" through subjugation and cruel onslaughts that turned the region into a physical and spiritual battleground.

Today, the struggle continues. This time the smell of oil, black gold of the modern age, feeds the hunger for power to control the oil that will gush forth from huge Caspian Sea reserves. In the next century the Caspian Basin is expected to produce more oil than the Gulf States. As a result, the Caucasuses could become more unstable than ever.

A Russian conscript, on duty during the war in his battle-worn tank, returns from an offensive near Grozny, the Chechen capital.

A concrete Soviet-style building in the heart of Grozny testifies to the artillery shelling which rocked the Chechen capital during the brutal siege of the city by the Russian army in 1994-1995.

When Shelala Rustamova was 9 years old, she collapsed after a shell hit near her village in Agdam region in Nagorno-Karabakh. Her condition continues to deteriorate. She lives immobile on her crib-bed in a one-room hut with her family at a refugee camp near Barda, Azerbaijan.

Alim (left) and Sadik (right) are Kurdish refugees from the former Soviet Azerbaijan Republic. They stand at the blackboard after lessons in their rundown school. On this day, only three students came to the school because it has no windows to keep out the cold.

A Chechen bride gathers water from a pipe in rural Chechnya. As one of her first wifely duties, she must carry water to the house of her husband, symbolizing the bringing of life to her new home. In the background, relatives fire guns to ward-off evil spirits.

A boy pauses during his work shoveling earth out of an open pit gold mine in the town of Durba. Because conflicts rage in the region, most mining companies have pulled out, leaving gold mining to locals who use the most rudimentary technology.

Three youth
same Lendu
with regular

37

Through a razor wire barrier, Congolese, some of them refugees from the fighting in Ituri province, sell items to Uruguayan troops stationed in Bunia as UN peacekeepers. The razor wire defines the perimeter of the Uruguayan camp.

A mother breastfeeds her child while having her hair styled at a refugee camp in Bunia.
In wartime, women and children are easily displaced.

Fishermen on Lake Kivu near Goma set their nets at dusk. The lake lies between Lake Tanganyika and Lake Albert. This Great Lakes Region, inside Rwanda, Burundi, the Congo and Uganda, has been the backdrop for genocide in Rwanda and the ongoing conflict.

"It is my hope that a portrait

of an exiled generation, and the

fragile future they represent,

will remind people of **what is at stake**."

TERU KUWAYAMA | pg 68

Strife | **CONSEQUENCE** | Insight

to give voice to history

Life on the ridge between two Sudans

After 20 years of civil war that killed 2 million people, the Sudanese government and the Sudan People's Liberation Movement in the country's south are one step away from a final peace agreement. A deal to equally split the country's newfound oil wealth was reached in early 2004, although the boundary separating north and south remains undefined. Three areas straddling the north-south divide are still disputed. One disputed part is the Nuba Mountain area, believed to be rich in oil.

The Nuba Mountain range is in the center of war-torn Sudan, Africa's largest country. The Nuba people took refuge in these mountains after they rebelled against Sharia (Islamic) law imposed in 1983 by the government in Khartoum and joined sides with rebellious southern Sudan, which is largely black animist and Christian in faith.

For decades, the Nuba were cut off from the rest of the world. This isolation caused serious hardship to a people already suffering because of war. They have been subjected to ethnic cleansing, forced Arabization, enslavement and endured repeated aerial bombings of their schools, hospitals, refugee camps, churches and other civilian targets.

In the absence of even the most basic necessities, these people faced suffering with strength and dignity and fought to maintain their ancient culture.

The anticipated flow of oil revenue will no doubt bring change to this unique culture, as its traditions engage the exigencies of a modern world.

Getting from Kauda to the markets in Kerker in the Nuba Mountains is almost always done on foot. Only a handful of vehicles move along the road, almost all belonging to the UN or non-governmental organizations.

PREVIOUS PAGE

Nuba return from work in the fields. Notwithstanding the war, the Nuba would come down from their makeshift homes in caves to cultivate farmland. There was no other way to provide food for their families, despite the danger of being caught by government soldiers.

The Nuba have practiced a form of wrestling since 2,800 B.C. Wrestling is an important Nuba tradition that has helped foster tribal and inter-tribal relationships. The Nuba have the longest unbroken martial arts tradition in the world.

NEXT PAGE

At Tira Limon in the Nuba Mountains, a young boy clambers on a rock above a peaceful-looking scene. In January, 2002, the Sudanese government and the southern rebels ended a 21-year civil war. In June, 2005, The UN took over monitoring the cease fire.

A battalion of soldiers performs maneuvers in the early morning at Kody in the Nuba Mountains of Sudan. In the post-war period, a new joint armed forces is being formed that is half Nuba and half government forces.

In Luera, Leila Kapirerno, 35, appears in partial shadow. In 1995, government soldiers captured
Leila's husband, tortured and killed him, leaving her with six children. Afterward, she hid in caves
until government soldiers forced her and other displaced people out with machine guns.

NEX T PAGE

In commemoration of the Nubas' struggle, the Sudan People's Liberation Army organizes celebrations at Tira Limon in the Nuba Mountains. The celebration has become a national holiday during which the Nuba practice ancient traditions including dance and wrestling.

A recently deceased man is prepared for a burial service. Tens of thousands of Nuba died in the last two decades. The civil war has claimed 2 million lives across the country, mainly from hunger and disease, and forced more than 4 million people from their homes.

Eyes skyward: relief comes to the Sudan

Mayandit is a village in Southern Sudan inhabited by Nuer people, one of the largest tribes in that country. In 2003, the people were suffering from the effects of a 20-year civil war. Although a ceasefire had been declared between the rebel Sudanese People's Liberation Army and the government of Sudan, this area still saw fighting daily. The lack of security, combined with a regional drought, had left the people of Mayandit with no food.

The World Food Programme (WFP), based in Rome, delivered food aid to the drought-stricken area. Almost all the food came from the U.S., which donated $78 million annually. Originally, the WFP estimated that 9,500 people in the area were at risk of starvation. However, when the food was being distributed, another 36,000 internally displaced people came to Mayandit, fleeing fighting in the neighboring town of Leer. A food drop that had been designed to sustain 9,500 people for one month had to be stretched to feed 45,000.

Mayandit sits atop one of the largest oil fields in East Africa and everyone wanted to control that oil. The villagers were caught in between the fighting and had nowhere to go. Every bomb dropped erased more of what remained of the villagers' way of life. Unable to raise crops or sustain their herds, many starved to death. Those who survived were completely reliant upon foreign aid for their food.

"Only the shirt you wear is what you come with," says Tong Buom. Buom and her 1-year-old grandson Bol Luong were displaced from their village of Tutnyang, after intense ground attacks and bombings by Government of Sudan Militias. The government of Sudan has adopted a scorched earth policy that displaces villagers from their land to allow for the exploration and drilling of oil.

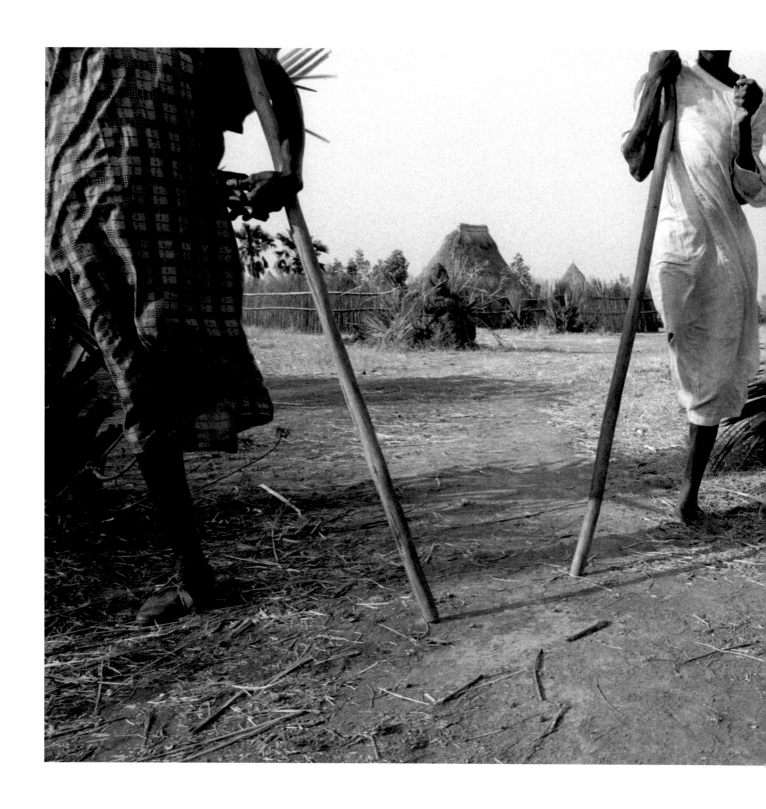

Amputees wait for the food distribution to begin outside of Mayandit. World Food Programme reaches women, children and disabled people in Southern Sudan who are those most adversely affected by the war. Because of the fighting in Western Upper Nile, the villagers have been unable to maintain cattle or crops.

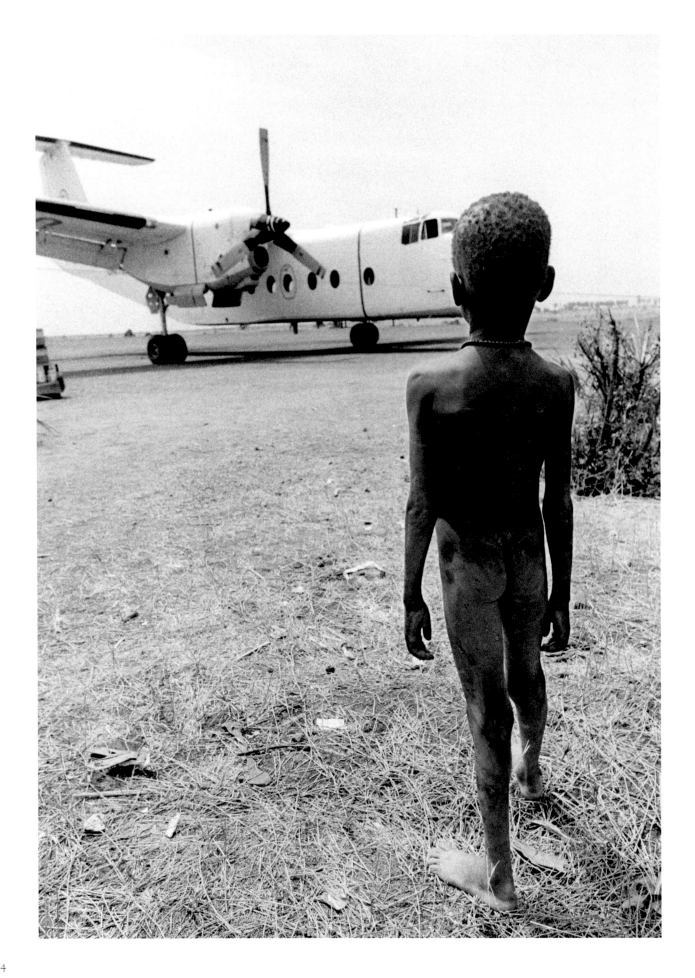

Students stand outside their classroom in Narus. In January 2003, the supply of food to students and teachers at the school had to be cancelled for several months.

A malnourished child watches as a World Food Programme Buffalo cargo plane gets ready to take off after bringing cooking oil to Mayandit.

Children watch as a World Food Programme C-130 cargo plane drops 50-kilogram sacks of corn. War and drought have left the people of Mayandit with no food and wholly dependent upon foreign aid. Almost all of the food comes from the U.S., which donates $78 million annually to Operation Lifeline Southern Sudan.

Exiled children learn Tibetan culture

In 1950, in the wake of the communist takeover of China, the Red Army swept into the isolated Tibetan plateau. More than 1 million Tibetans died in the subsequent "peaceful liberation" of their isolated nation. At the time, Tibet's head of state was a teenage monk, the 14th Dalai Lama.

After a decade of Chinese occupation, the Dalai Lama and some 10,000 followers fled across the Himalayas to refugee settlements in India. Each year, thousands more followed, and today, more than 150,000 Tibetans live as stateless refugees in Nepal and India. Many of the great monasteries of Tibet have been resurrected in India, where Tibetan Buddhism may be freely studied and practiced.

The Tibetan's Children's Village (TCV) project began more than 40 years ago following the first exodus of refugees from Tibet. At that time, the Dalai Lama assigned his sister to care for some 50 Tibetan orphans whose parents had died on the trek across the mountains. That first group home eventually developed into a network of schools, lodges, and orphanages that now educate and care for some 15,000 Tibetan children. Each year, approximately 1,000 additional children are delivered from Tibet to the TCV system to be raised with a "Tibetan Education." Only in exile are the children free to learn their own language and history and to practice their faith.

Tenzing, a "trulku," believed to be the reincarnation of a high lama, celebrates his fifth birthday at a party in Bylakuppe, in southern India. Restrictions against children entering the monasteries of Tibet made it impossible for children to pursue the faith of their families and people.

Bylakuppe, located in the south Indian state of Karnataka, was the first permanent settlement established by the Tibetan government in exile in 1960. Bylakuppe is now home to more than 15,000 stateless Tibetan exiles, with the Sera Je Monastery housing more than 3,000 monks.

The new Sera Je Monastery in southern India is the largest center of Tibetan Buddhist learning in the world. Prior to the Chinese occupation, the original Sera Je Monastery in Tibet was one of the world's largest monasteries of any faith, with almost 10,000 monks.

A fisherman in Kribi drags his pirogue through the surf. Fish stocks dropped to almost nothing after the pipeline was laid. More than half of the fishermen have abandoned fishing.

"I believe documenting and thereby

heightening awareness of this

vanishing culture will contribute to

its survival and help to

preserve the wealth of its traditions."

AMI VITALE | pg 124

Strife | Consequence | **INSIGHT**

to give voice to cultural differences

Conflicts of culture in a changed world

A flag is a symbol. But what it symbolizes to one segment of society may be the opposite of what it symbolizes to another. Perhaps not surprisingly after all, it turns out that the symbolism behind a flag is relative and is in the eye of the beholder.

Nowhere is the divide over the truth and beauty of a flag wider than in South Carolina, where the Civil War began 145 years ago, and where a state of incivility exists to this day, fueled in part by the continuing debate over the public display of a piece of red and blue cloth known as the Confederate flag. This same emblem that symbolizes one man's pride in his Southern roots reminds another man of a legacy of racial prejudice. The scrap of fabric that honors ancestors who fought and died for the Confederacy dishonors the descendants of the system of slavery that the Confederacy fought to perpetuate. The symbol of one man's heritage is emblematic of another man's history of enslavement.

The story goes beyond the controversy over the flag and explores the people behind the intense debate; those who have suffered long under acts of oppression, and the descendants of soldiers who fought for the preservation of a way of life they held dear. These are people who have shared a native soil but have not shared the same ideology.

Change comes slowly in the South, and tradition means something different to every person.

Pride in the Confederate flag as a symbol of the South is so strong that some people not only fly the flag, they also wrap themselves in it. At 8 a.m. at Darlington Raceway, a fan in rebel attire climbs atop his flag-adorned truck, and awaits the beginning of the race, hours away.

Jacque Gerard of Camden, S.C., holds up her end of a giant Confederate flag at the State House during one of the many pro-flag demonstrations. The State House is a major site for frequent demonstrations, both for and against the flag.

Scraps of wood and containers of gasoline are left over from a KKK rally held near the
Lexington, S.C., home of a Klan Grand Dragon. The KKK of the New South combines family
picnics with traditional cross burnings, a trademark of the Klan since the first burning in 1915.

Sharecroppers and recently freed slaves built the St. Paul Campground 130 years ago. It stands today near Harleyville, S.C. Those original families gathered there annually for a week, following successful harvest seasons, to reunite and praise and share their harvests. Descendants from across the U.S. still come here, keeping the tradition alive.

Civil War reenactment is a big business throughout the South, but especially in South Carolina.
Jane Kroll, dressed as a Confederate widow, puts her arms around a young spectator at Battery
Park, Charleston, S.C., during a reenactment of the battle of Ft. Wagner

Chernobyl's children suffer from radiation

On April 26, 1986, reactor number four at the Chernobyl Nuclear Power Station exploded on the border of the Ukraine and Belarus. The resulting fire burned out of control for five days and spewed more than 50 tons of radioactive fallout across Belarus. For several days, the government denied the accident had happened, and allowed the people in the Gomel region of Belarus to linger in the radiation. When the dangerous truth came slowly to light, schools were closed, thousands of villages were abandoned, prime cattle were slaughtered and huge factories were shut down. Even today, a large portion of the land is considered uninhabitable.

Although many of the sick were not even born at the time of the nuclear accident, 10 years after the blast the radiation's fallout has become their legacy. The cause of their illnesses is hard to trace, harder yet to prove. But the rise in the number of cancer cases in this region is too great for any other conclusion: it has to be the radiation that is sickening these children.

Many doctors and radiation specialists say that it is too early to know everything about the long-term effects of Chernobyl.

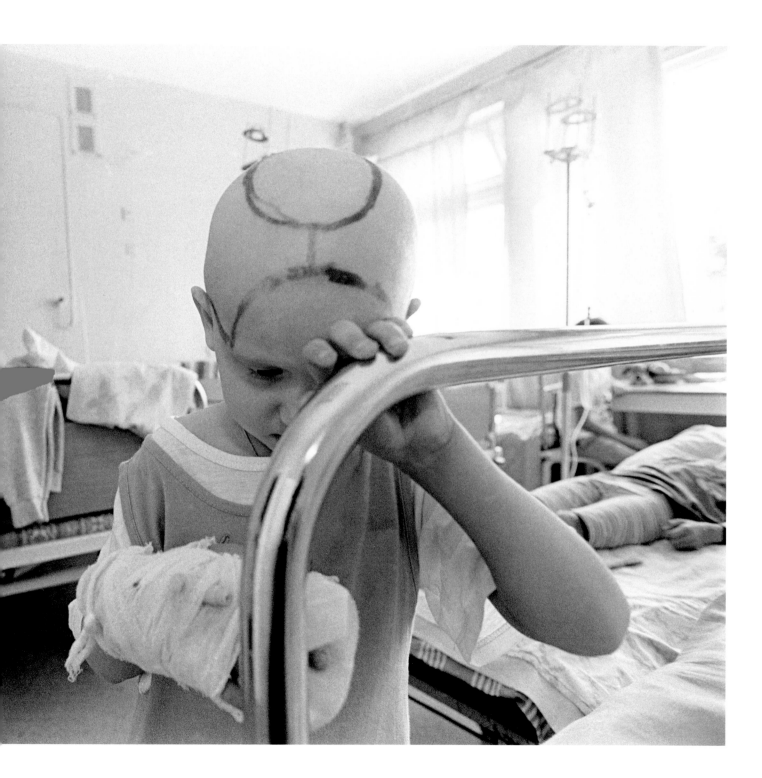

Four-year-old Andrey Sabirov from Gomel is treated for leukemia at the Gomel Regional Clinical Hospital in Belarus. A 1995 United Nations report stated that the Chernobyl disaster caused a 100 percent increase in the incidence of cancer and leukemia in children.

Doctors at the Gomel Regional Clinical Hospital begin to operate on tiny 3-month-old Olga Danilenko, who was born with multiple birth defects. A 1995 United Nations report stated that the Chernobyl disaster caused a 250 percent increase in congenital birth deformities.

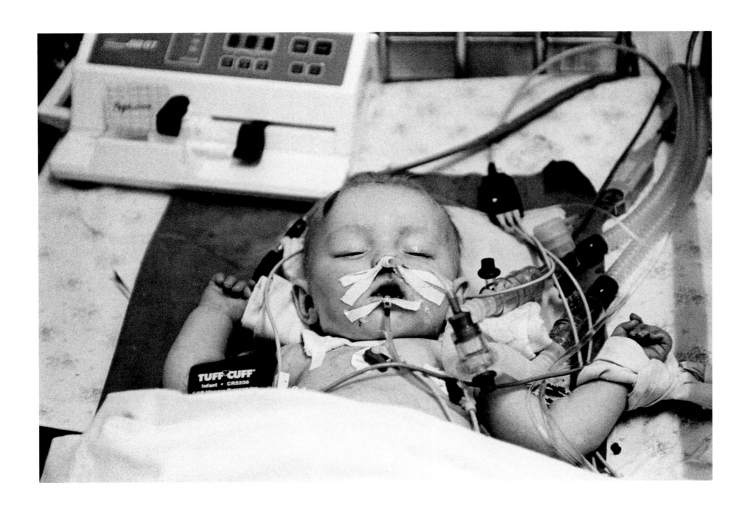

Vova Aksenov, a 5-month-old from the city of Minsk, is connected to life support at the intensive care unit of the Children's Regional Hospital in Minsk, Belarus. Vova was premature.

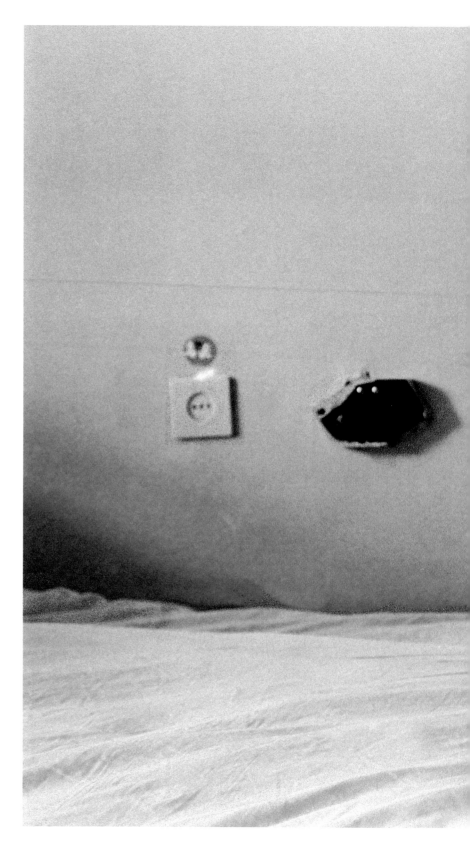

Nastya Dolgovevets, 2, from Slutsk in the Minsk region, was diagnosed with a wrist tumor at the Children's Division of the Oncology Research Institute in Minsk, Belarus. The marks on her head are from iodine that the doctors dabbed on mysterious spots.

When Dimitry Maidiuk, 7, arrived in Cuba from the Ukraine two years ago, he was not able to walk. Now he runs, swims and plays like other children his own age. When he is 14, he will return to Cuba for more surgery to make the brace he wears unnecessary. Irina Kovaliova, the photographer here, is only seven, yet she has arthritis.

104

Cuban doctors treat Chernobyl children

In 1996, in Tarara, Cuba, on the tenth anniversary of the Chernobyl nuclear disaster, children continued to receive treatment at a Caribbean resort near Havana. There, expert medical care and the soothing effects of the tropical sun and clean air have helped cure many children suffering from effects of radiation poisoning.

A team of Cuban doctors has turned the resort into a treatment center for children with hair loss, skin disorders, cancer, leukemia and other illnesses attributed to the radioactivity unleashed by the reactor meltdown that occurred years before these children were born. Since Chernobyl, incidences of childhood thyroid cancer have increased 30-fold. Doctors say children are especially susceptible to thyroid damage from radiation because their thyroids are smaller than an adult's. Thyroid cancer is one of the disorders that has been directly linked to the Chernobyl accident. Scientists do not know, however, whether hair loss is caused by radioactive pollution or post-traumatic stress.

Since it opened in 1990, the camp has hosted more than 18,000 children from Ukraine, Belarus and Russia, the former territories of the Soviet Union most affected by the contamination that spread over an area the size of New York. Despite Cuba's economic crisis, the government provides free medical care as well as food, housing and schools for about 150 children rotated in and out of Tarara every few months. Recreation is as much a part of the cure as the medical treatment, Cuban doctors say.

A Chinese wedding starts at the home of the bride and groom. Maggie waits in the car while Sang rounds up the wedding party for the trip to his parent's flat in Peckham. There, the couple will be honored with a tea ceremony.

A cultural struggle for Asian immigrants

People in the West may pore over media accounts of business in China and Japan or politics in Vietnam and Hong Kong. Yet, despite increased cultural awareness of the people living in East Asia, westerners may know little about immigrants from those same countries who may be living as close as next door. One such group of East Asians who now call the West home consists of brothers Jackie, Hui, Mingh, and Sang and Sang's wife, Maggie. They are the first East Asians in their families to grow up in Europe — Great Britain, to be exact. Their story is one shared by many.

Newlyweds Maggie and Sang purchased their home in Barking, East London, four months before their wedding. Maggie works as a waitress in a Chinese restaurant in the Docklands and Sang works as a mechanical engineer. Two of Sang's brothers worked in the family business — a Chinese take-out restaurant — to provide support for Sang and his middle brother, so they both could complete engineering degrees.

As a result of their surroundings, the western influence can be seen in the group's style of dress, choice of profession, lifestyles and habits. But, as East Asians in western Europe, they struggle to maintain their ancestral heritage against the onslaught of a foreign culture. For them, the process of adopting a new homeland is a process of adapting to a new world.

A challenging life for Oaxacan children

Children on the streets of Oaxaca, Mexico, dwell in poverty and live without direction, some as outcasts sleeping under a city bridge. Many have spent time in jail. Even more use drugs—sniffing solvents and glue or smoking marijuana. Living by their wits, they clean car windows at stop lights, shine shoes, act as street performers and beg for tips.

The Oaxaca Streetchildren Grassroots organization reports that many of these children are the sole support for their families.

No one knows exactly how many street children there are, but at almost any hour of the day, 30 or 40 will be in the city's central plaza. Recently, small but organized gangs of children have appeared and intimidated others, making life on the streets even meaner for those who must live there.

Gang members in Oaxaca, Mexico, call this teenager El Moreno (loosely translated, "the Dark One"). He is known as a strong and fierce street fighter. Playing against type, he wears a mask as if he is the one who's afraid and in hiding.

Prisoners with AIDs protest treatment

In September 1992, HIV-positive prisoners protested conditions at Vacaville, California's main prison hospital for men, by refusing to take their medications. As many as 150 of the 330 inmates living in the facility's separate HIV unit participated. More than 400 men died of AIDS in the prison from 1986 to 1996.

It was also clear that the doctors were continually frustrated by the prison bureaucracy's indifference to patients' needs. All three left. Dr. Maisonet, an infection control specialist at the minimum security federal prison in Pleasanton, said of his decision to resign, "It hurt a lot to leave, but we were faced with an increasing number of patients and a decreasing amount of resources. I would have had to practice medicine at a level below the standard of care, and I wouldn't have been satisfied."

In 1991-92, prisoners organized outside supporters who appealed to the state legislature. Since then, a hospice was set up, a peer education program began and pastoral care services for the dying were expanded and strengthened inside the HIV unit at Vacaville.

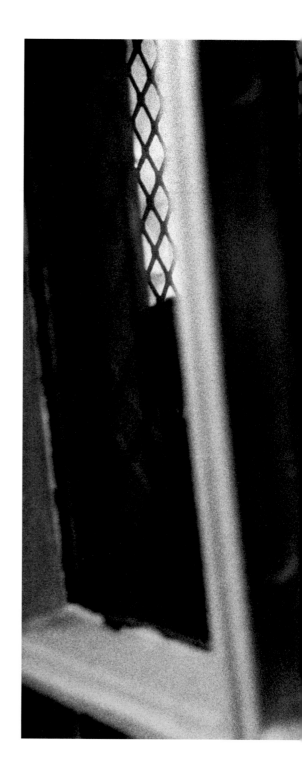

A Vacaville Prison inmate watches television in an isolation unit for HIV positive prisoners which inmates called the "Death Ward." HIV positive inmates who had voluntarily tested for HIV were removed from the prison's general population and placed in the isolation unit.

Inmate-workers are moved from one field to the next, never far from the watchful eyes of prison guards on horseback, armed with both pistol and rifle. Many inmates, including those imprisoned for drug crimes, are considered nonviolent offenders.

Old prison ways,
new prison reform

Texas has the largest prison system of any state in the nation. At the end of 2004, the Lone Star State held more than 168,000 prisoners behind bars. Texas Department of Criminal Justice statistics show that more than one in five inmates is serving time on drug-related charges and many more are said to be seriously addicted to alcohol or other drugs.

Rising drug use in all segments of society has raised new questions about how addicted offenders should be handled and whether it is better to spend money on incarceration or rehabilitation. Texas, long branded as a state with one of the most archaic prison systems in the country, is now one of a handful of states with a large-scale drug rehabilitation program for felony offenders. In the early '90s, the state launched the "Texas Initiative," an ambitious program of prison-based drug and alcohol treatment. More recently, changes in the political leadership resulted in scaled back or halted program development but not before seeing initially encouraging results in the area of lower recidivism rates and reduced drug use among successful program graduates.

Forgotten Black Okies of Central California

One of Dorothea Lange's famous photographs—
"Ditched, Stalled, and Stranded, San Joaquin Valley,
California"—now graces a U.S. postage stamp. This
picture, along with books such as John Steinbeck's
Grapes of Wrath, has come to define the story of
"Okie" migrants of the Great Depression. But these
works create an incomplete picture of this chapter
of American history and have contributed to the
widespread, but false, perception that Dust Bowl
migration, one of the largest population shifts ever to
occur in the U.S., was exclusively a white journey.

About 10,000 self-described Black Okies still live
in several remote rural enclaves scattered amid the
cotton fields of Central California. Though some
50,000 of them came to the San Joaquin Valley during
the Depression and worked side by side with real-life
counterparts to Steinbeck's fictional Joad family, no
books or photographs ever documented their lives.
Today, their struggling communities represent tattered
remnants of this forgotten chapter of America's rural life.

Present-day descendants of the Black Okies live
in conditions that seem lifted straight out of the
sharecropper South. Even the younger generation lives
in the shadow of the past. Hallie Jones, born in 1960,
chops cotton in one of the same fields where her father
worked over a half-century ago. She has inherited her
father's hardscrabble life.

A third-generation resident of Teviston plays on an abandoned farm truck south of town. Black migrants often settled on some of the worst land in rural California, making farming difficult. The area surrounding Teviston is scarred with drifts of alkali, which are visible throughout the area.

Henry Clay, born in Arkansas, migrated as a boy with his family to rural California. Now in his sixties and suffering from ill health, he spends much of his time fishing. With the mechanization of cotton farming, families like his are no longer needed in California's farm fields.

James Dixon, 96, stands in front of his home in Teviston, a town founded by black sharecroppers fleeing Dust Bowl states. Today, just a handful of the original migrants remain, scattered throughout a few remote and impoverished rural enclaves in California's San Joaquin Valley.

Seen through a dirty window from a neighboring house, a parishioner, dressed all in white for Communion Sunday, enters the social hall following services at the House of Prayer, a Pentecostal church in Teviston. Only a handful of these rural black churches remain.

Couple shares Navajo lifestyle

The Navajo Nation is the largest Indian tribe in the U.S. with more than 250,000 members. Their 7,400 square mile reservation extends from northwestern New Mexico into Arizona and Utah. It is larger than many states, including West Virginia.

Because of harsh conditions on the reservation, many Navajos have moved into local towns where they can enjoy more modern conveniences. But, being away from the land makes it difficult to pass on Navajo culture to their young people.

Ashiikee, an 80-year-old Navajo man, met his wife, Yil Ni Bah, at a squaw dance when he was in third grade. The 85-year-old Navajo woman cared for her semi-blind husband in a typical Navajo dwelling, called a hogan, on the reservation in Carson, New Mexico.

The hogan consists of one large round room with a fireplace or stove in the middle. Yil Ni Bah has lived her whole life on the reservation. Ashiikee served in the Navy during WWII. He was one of the "code talkers" who used the Navajo language to send messages which the Japanese were never able to decode.

The couple lived a quiet life on the reservation. Most days, they enjoyed listening to Navajo music on the radio and tapping out the rhythms on the kitchen table.

Yil Ni Bah, 85, tends the fire in the stove that warms the hogan, a typical Navajo dwelling she and her husband, Ashiikee, 80, share on the reservation in Carson, New Mexico. The couple met at a reservation dance.

"Swing me," 6-year-old Lucy Sherman begs family friend Sara Jean Schweitzer. The California residents were visitors at an annual reunion that draws hundreds of former farm members. The two met on a hot July day on a country road that leads to the swimming hole at The Farm community in rural Tennessee.

Kids adopt ideas of communal parents

Early in 1970, a counterculture fleet of wildly painted school buses sailed east from San Francisco's Haight-Ashbury district to the rolling hills of Tennessee. In a world filled with strife and political disillusionment during the Vietnam War, these pilgrims believed that harmonious living, expressed through a "do-good" philosophy, could bring about holistic change. Their collective motto: "Out to save the world."

Within a year, the 250 founders had firmly sunk roots in the Southern soil, started families and named their new community "The Farm." Over the next decade, The Farm became the country's most famous commune. Sharing a philosophy of pacifism, vegetarianism, natural childbirth, marriage and family, the farmers were dedicated to bringing forth peace.

The goal was Utopia but the commune fell far short of that dream. In 1983, The Farm disintegrated, brought down by poverty, debt, and disillusionment. Nonetheless, it had produced a generation that was raised communally, and had experienced first-hand the benefits of true cooperation, respect for the land and earth and the necessity of peace. Now, more than 25 years after the founding of America's largest "hippie commune," the community's second generation—500 strong—is coming of age in the material world their parents voluntarily rejected. These children and their parents gather annually in Tennessee at a reunion of former residents of The Farm.

Dembel Jumpora is nestled in the eastern part of Guinea Bissau. The climate is hot and humid but by the end of the dry season, little water will be found above ground. The children take advantage of the rains to enjoy a day of swimming.

124

Muslim nomads maintain culture

The Fulani, who once crisscrossed the continent of Africa tending their precious herds of cattle, was a civilization known for its constant movement. This nomadic existence spun the threads of a rich social fabric of tradition and ritual that endures to this day. In the West African country of Guinea Bissau, the former nomads have settled in the village of Dembel Jumpora, become farmers and now struggle to adapt to a world that has rudely intruded upon them.

Unlike most other ethnic tribes in Guinea Bissau, the Fulani are Muslim. Village life is structured according to Islamic traditions including performing male and female circumcision, praying five times a day, following the Islamic calendar and practicing polygamy.

The inclusion of local beliefs and traditions produces a brand of Islam that is unique to its area and its people. From the belief in tree spirits to the use of traditional medicine or "voodoo," the mixing of cultures that took place centuries earlier has produced a society that blends a unique spiritual universe with an often brutal daily existence in the physical world.

To an outsider, the village may appear to be a place where a people, living simply, struggle to survive. While that perception is partially valid, the social hierarchy and politics existing among members of the tribe are far more complex than in most modern western societies.

Boys play soccer underneath an enormous Bontang tree. Though the Fulani are a Muslim tribe, they also believe that this tree has a spirit. Mixing animist beliefs and Islamic law creates a society that has a great respect for the land, the supernatural world and the laws of God.

Children eat the staple diet of rice from a communal bowl. At the end of the dry season, there is little food and many will have only one meal of rice each day.

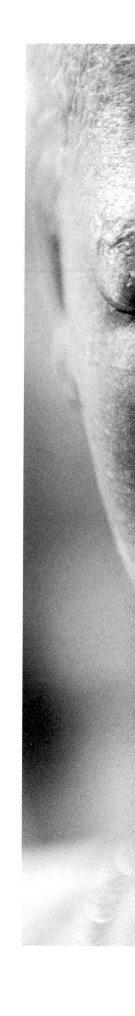

Awa Balde, 5, cries after being circumcised. Once a girl passes through the rite of circumcision, she is considered a respectable prospect for marriage. A future husband will sometimes pay a dowry to claim a bride before she becomes a teenager.

"Through your work, you really can **put these places on the map**, get people interested in **places and stories** they would have never been exposed to."

IN CONCLUSION

promote global understanding through photojournalism

MATT BLACK

Matt Black is a California native who has photographed the region extensively. His work on the Black Okies of rural California was a finalist for the Pulitzer Prize in Feature Photography. He has been honored by many grants and awards including one from the National Endowment for the Arts. Matt holds a B.A. in U.S. and Latin American history from San Francisco State University.

pg 114 | Migrant Sharecroppers

MARCUS BLEASDALE

Marcus Bleasdale spent six years covering the brutal conflict in the Democratic Republic of Congo and published this work in *One Hundred Years of Darkness.* He has received several first prizes in Pictures of the Year and NPPA competitions. In 2005, Marcus was named Magazine Photographer of the Year by POYi. He was previously UNICEF Photographer of the Year (2004).

pg 74 | Chad-Cameroon Pipeline

HEIDI BRADNER

Heidi Bradner was born and raised in Alaska. She was based in Eastern Europe and Russia in the 1990s and covered the collapse of the former USSR and the related wars in that region. Her photographs of the protracted war in Chechnya won the Leica Medal of Excellence and a Mother Jones International Fund for Documentary Photography Grant. Her most recent work concentrates on the nomadic reindeer herders of Siberia.

pg 26 | Chechnya

RAMÓN JIMÉNEZ CUEN

Ramón Jimenez Cuen was born in 1976 in Oaxaca, Mexico, and currently makes his home there. His book, "Brothers Under the Bridge," about street children in Oaxaca, was published in 2001 and his photographs on that same subject have been displayed in Mexico and in London. He owns a small company dedicated to photography, web design and video production.

pg 108 | Oaxaca, Mexico Outcasts

JAN DAGO

Jan Dago, was born in Ry, Denmark, in 1964. After 10 years of freelancing around the world, he returned to Denmark in 2004 to work as staff photographer for *Morgenavisen Jyllands-Posten* doing assignments in Denmark and abroad. He is the winner of the World Press Photo, First Prize General News, for his work documenting war in Sierra Leone.

pg 10 | Sierra Leone Conflict

ELENA FAVA EMERSON

Elena Fava Emerson was born in Milan, Italy, and gravitated first to a career in fashion photography. After moving to San Francisco, she reinvented herself as a photojournalist, documenting life through a camera lens. She attended State University of Milan and San Francisco State University where she photographed Native American reservations for her thesis. She is currently a freelance photojournalist and is cofounder of the on-line magazine, *After5media*.

pg 120 | Native American Reservation

SUSANNA FROHMAN

Susanna Frohman is a professional photojournalist who took her first photographs with her father's Nikon at the age of nine. She currently works at the *San Jose* (Calif.) *Mercury News* and previously was on the staff at the *San Francisco Chronicle*. Frohman has received grants from the the National Geographic Books division and Ohio University's School of Visual Communication, where she graduated. Frohman grew up on "The Farm," the subject of her story in this book.

LAURA KLEINHENZ

Laura Kleinhenz is an award-winning documentary photographer. A graduate of the University of North Carolina School of Journalism and Mass Communication, she has covered Latin America and the Southeastern U.S. for *Time, Newsweek* and *The New York Times*. Her photo essays include "Chernobyl Children in Cuba" and "Sex and the Senior World: An Exploration of Dating among the Aging."

TERU KUWAYAMA

Teru Kuwayama is an independent documentary photographer and a regular contributor to *Time, Newsweek, Fortune,* and *Outside.* In recent years, his work has focused on the aftermath of war and disaster in Iraq, Afghanistan and South Asia. He holds a BFA from State University of New York, Albany, and co-authored "The Freedom: Shadows and Hallucinations in Occupied Iraq."

pg 68 | Tibetan Refugees

WESLEY LAW

Wesley Law was born in St. Louis, Mo., in 1977 and graduated from Syracuse University with a B.A. in Photography in 2000. Law worked for the *St. Louis Post-Dispatch* in 1998, then moved to London later that year to begin documenting the lives of East Asian immigrants. He now lives in New York and works in commercial photography and independent films.

pg 106 | London's East Asian Immigrants

ROGER LEMOYNE

Roger Lemoyne graduated from Concordia University in Montreal, where he is based, with a degree in cinema production and worked in film and music before becoming a full-time photographer. He has covered the crisis in the Horn of Africa (Somalia, Ethiopia, Sudan) and worked primarily on international issues. Lemoyne received third place Magazine Photographer of the Year in POYi in 2004.

pg 34 | Effects of Conflict on Children

JOHN MCCONNICO

John McConnico, a Pulitzer Prize and World Press Photo award-winning photojournalist, works worldwide as a freelance photographer. He formerly photographed and edited for the Associated Press. As a master's degree candidate at the University of Texas, he used his camera to explore the dysfunctional Texas prison system. He is currently working on in-depth features and photo essays in Europe from his home in Denmark.

pg 112 | Alternative Prisons

DARCY PADILLA

Darcy Padilla is a documentary photographer based in San Francisco. She has chronicled the lives of the poor in the U.S. since 1992. Darcy's project on poverty was selected for the first UNAIDS exhibition in Geneva. She has received awards from the Open Society and a John Simon Guggenheim Fellowship. Her work has appeared in *Graphis, Harpers Bazaar, Life Magazine, The New York Times* and *The Washington Post*.

pg 110 | Prison Conditions

PEGGY PEATTIE

Peggy Peattie has worked at the *San Diego (Calif.) Union-Tribune* since 1998. She has worked at newspapers in Columbia, S.C., Torrance, Calif., and Long Beach, Calif. She has a master's degree in Visual Communication from Ohio University. She won Greater Los Angeles Press Photographer of the Year five consecutive times and the 2000 National Press Photographer's Region 10 Photographer of the Year.

pg 88 | Confederate Flag Controversy

EZRA SHAW

Ezra Shaw graduated from Syracuse University in 1996 with a degree in photojournalism, and has traveled the world working on projects ranging from the Australian Open to a series of portraits at children's hospitals near Chernobyl. He now works as a freelance photographer in New York and has covered the winter and summer Olympics, World Series, NBA Finals, Stanley Cup Finals, Super Bowl and U.S. Open.

pg 98 | Chernobyl's Legacy

AMI VITALE

Ami Vitale attended the University of North Carolina and worked for the Associated Press as a picture editor in New York and Washington, D.C. She has since worked in Eastern Europe, Africa and Barcelona. She found her Alexia project when visiting her sister who was in Africa in the Peace Corps. She has lived in the Czech Republic and is now based in India.

pg 124 | Muslim Culture in West Africa

JUSTIN YURKANIN

Justin Yurkanin was born in Cincinnati, Ohio, in 1980, and has lived all over the world. He graduated from Syracuse University in 2002 and works for the *St. Augustine* (Fla.) *Record*. He has covered stories in Sudan and the aftermath of Hurricane Katrina in Bay St. Louis, Miss. Yurkanin is currently working on a story about adoption in Haiti.

pg 58 | Coping with Civil Strife in Sudan

FRANCESCO ZIZOLA

©LEO CARBOTTA

Francesco Zizola was born in Rome in 1962 and has worked as a photographer covering international news for major newspapers and magazines since 1986. His work has been recognized with numerous awards including World Press Photo awards in 1995, 1997, 1998, 2002 and 2005. He claimed World Press Photo of the Year in 1996 for a photo documenting the tragedy of land mines in Angola.

pg 46 | People of the Nuba Mountains

1991   Tamara Voninski, Ronald Amstutz, Tory Read, Darcy Padilla, Michael Lutsky

1992   Dan McComb, John McConnico, Teresa Hurteau, Sean Gallup, Jay Talbott

1993   Liu Xin, Ian Martin, Torsten Kjellstrand, Huy Nguyen, Greg Latza

1994   Jenafer Gillingham, Kerstin Hacker, Kim Ritzenthaler, Matt Black, Shelley Eades

1995   Laura M. Kleinhenz, Elisa Maple, Joseph John Kotlowski, Ted S. Warren, Craig Fritz

1996   Ezra O. Shaw, Michel Fortier, Stefanie Boyar, Meryl Schenker, Michelle Mott

1997   Rami Maalouf, Chris Stanford, Barry Gutierrez, Ryan Anson, Susanna Frohman; Peggy Peattie*

1998   Eric Grigorian, Shannon Taggart, Christopher Lane, Brian Finke; Heidi Bradner*

1999   Melissa Brooke Lyttle, Wesley Law, Max Becherer, Angie Jimenez, Logan Wallace; Teru Kuwayama*

2000   Logan Mock-Bunting, James Prichard, Cara Van Leuven, Elena Fava Emerson, Kristen Schmid, Julia Crum; Ami C. Vitale*

2001   Tom Mason, Ramón Jiménez Cuen, J.D. Perkins, Stephanie Keith, Nicole Tarver; Jan Dago*

2002   Justin J. Yurkanin, Daniel Pepper, Roberto Westbrook, Zachary R. Ornitz, Jamie Rose; Kai Wiedenhofer*

2003   Christopher J. Capozziello, Jamie Cohen, Lori Duff, Danny Gawlowski, Leila Navidi; Matt Black*

2004   Marie Arago, Mark Murrmann, Andres Gonzalez, Lisa Hornstein; Roger Lemoyne;* Francesco Zizola*

2005   Erika Schultz, Jessa Buchalter, Julie Ann Peters, Andrew Henderson, Laura Elizabeth Pohl; Marcus Bleasdale*

        * professional winners

Judges   Vincent Alabiso, Nancy Andrews, J. Bruce Baumann, Renee Byer, Jodi Cobb, Cotton Coulson, Harry DiOrio, Mark Edelson, Macduff Everton, Kevin Gilbert, Robert Gilka, Mary Ann Golon, Thomas Graves, David Griffin, Kari Rene Hall, John Kaplan, Torsten Kjellstrand, Yunghi Kim, Bob Lynn, Carol McKay, Michele McNally, Clem Murray, Larry Nighswander, Jim Preston, Mike Smith, Susan Smith, Jodie Steck and Joe Traver.

ACKNOWLEDGMENTS

It is with grateful hearts that we thank:

David Sutherland, photography professor at the Newhouse School at Syracuse University, the anchor of our ship.

Vincent Alabiso, chair of the Alexia Foundation board of directors, for assembling our board and setting our course for the future.

The S.I. Newhouse School of Public Communications at Syracuse University for providing a home for the Alexia Competitions.

Bob Gilka, who has judged the "Alexia" 13 times and is affectionately called the "godfather" of the Alexia Competitions.

Daile Kaplan, Alexia Foundation board member, vice president/director of photographs, Swann Galleries, NYC, curator of the Foundation exhibit at the UN in 2006.

Michelle Stephenson, Alexia Foundation board member, director of photography, *Time* Magazine, NYC, liaison for the book, "Eyes on the World."

Eliane Laffont, Alexia Foundation board member for giving us international exposure by taking us to "Visa Pour L'Image" in Perpignan, France.

Sherri Taylor and her senior graphics class at The Newhouse School at Syracuse University for their vision and commitment in designing this book.

Bill Marr, *National Geographic* executive editor, who shepherded this book to completion in record time.

Nirelle Galson, administrator, Syracuse University Department of International Programs Abroad, for supporting our winners at the London Centre.

David Tomlin, Alexia Foundation board member, for his invaluable legal counsel.

Richard Krim, Alexia Foundation board member, for his guidance and financial expertise.

Our son, George, and our daughter, Ariadne, for their singular devotion and commitment to the memory of their sister.

— Peter & Aphrodite Tsairis

PICTURE EDITORS

Michele Stephenson, director of photography, *Time* Magazine
Vincent Alabiso, president of VJA, Inc.
Jim Dooley, former director of photography, *Newsday*
Daile Kaplan, vice-president and director of photographs, Swann Galleries, Inc., New York
Eliane Laffont, editorial director of Hachette Filipacchi Media
Nancy Lee, vice president of business development, *The New York Times*
    All are Alexia Foundation Board members.

DESIGN TEAM

Sherri Taylor, professor of graphic arts at the Newhouse School at Syracuse University
Senior graphic arts majors: Camille Baker, Christine Buerkle, Amy Citron, Jen Dawes,
    Tarynne Goldenberg, Jill Haydinger, Leyla Heckrotte, Libby Hemming, Katie Hollenbeck,
    Brendan Kneram, Kathy Nguyen, Elie Stephenson, Katie Thompson, Yasmin Vahdatpour.

DESIGN CONSULTANT

Bill Marr, executive editor, *National Geographic*

COPY EDITOR

Elaine Ayers, director of Central Legal Research, School of Law, University of North Dakota

DIGITAL IMAGING

Sung Park, professor of photojournalism at the Newhouse School at Syracuse University